MEMORY TREASURE

ADEELA SHAIKH & ZAIRA ALI

ISBN 979-888546568-7

Contents

Contents

Contents

Acknowledgements

I'm the compiler of this book want to thanks our readers who are reading this book, our family members for supporting us,our Kashish Publication, our editor, God for helping us in this journey and special thanks to the most important ones, our co-authors, for sharing your moments that you lived.

Thanks to each and every co-author and member of our "Memory Treasure". We are blessed to have you in our lives. Without you, Memory Treasure would not have been successfully completed and once again a big thanks to our readers for choosing this book

Disclaimer

This anthology is a fiction. Anthology "Memory Treasure" is an ideal mix of the writers gathered from a gathering of excellent essayists from everywhere in the whole world. All the writings published in this book are originally written by the respective mentioned co authors.

This book doesn't intend to disrespect any community, caste, religion,creed, nationality and gender. Compiler and publisher would not be responsible, if in case the content is plagiarized the respective co-authors will be entirely responsible for the misbehavior.

About Us

Kashish Publications is a growing platform for all the budding writers to fulfill their dream. It is founded by Kashish Soni,a budding writer who believe that writing is the magic to heal one's heart.

"YOU DREAM,WE ACCOMPLISHED!"

You can contact us for solo publishing or for compiling a one of our own.

Instagram id- @kashish_publications

Gmail- sonikashish004@gmail.com

About The Project Head

He is Mr. Krishna Bagdi. He hails from Madhya Pradesh. He is an entrepreneur and a digital business consultant.
Founder of Dream World Publication and Helping Hand Foundation. He has a keen interest in writing and photography.
"When you have fire of dreams in your eyes, I am serving you all here so that each writer would be appreciated when someone reads a book."

About The Compiler- Adeela Shaikh

Adeela Shaikh is 17 years old intermediate student at SSSG, Aligarh Muslim University who is pursuing 12th grade in Humanities stream. Born in UP and currently live in Mau (Uttar Pradesh).Her Hobbies are writing, reading, social working, watching horror movies and web series. She writes from heart. She was fond of reading books since childhood. She believes that do what makes ourselves happy and no matter what's the situation or scenario comes in life, just believe in yourself and keep loving yourself. She believes that writing is a very good way to express the feelings what one can't speak in situation word. Being co-author of 100+ anthologies. Adeela is currently working her upcoming anthologies. Her good numbers of short stories and poem has been published at different sources. She's compiler of Eternal Blue Sky Publication , Kashish Publication, Starnik Publication,Lost Pearl Publication and Jehova Jireh

Publication.

Today, she's an aspiring IAS and dreamer of world famous story teller.

About The Compiler- Zaira Ali

Zaira Ali is an intermediate student at SSSG, Aligarh Muslim University . Born in Bihar and currently lives in Bihar Sharif (Nalanda). She is studious and natural learner .She is a strong believer in the power of positive thinking. She is social worker and loves to help others. She is passionate towards reading since childhood. Especially the motivational and empowerment as well romance genre.Thus keen interest in book has turned her into innovative and creative thinker.Today, she is an aspiring IAS ,social worker and dreamer of famous story writer to bring changes in society.

Compiler's Desk

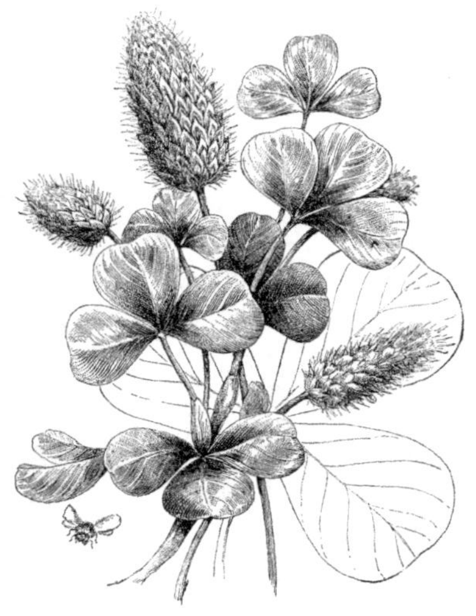

1. Adeela Shaikh

HAUNTED NIGHT

The night was dark, the moon was also hidden behind the clouds, causing darkness all around.

This thing happened when I was only 16 years old. Then I was alone in the house. My parents went to Florida to attend the wedding. My school was going on due to which I could not go with my parents and I had to stay at home.

New York street number 132 , was very deserted. Everyone in New York is busy with their own work. I was a student and used to spend most of my time studying. When I went to sleep after studying, it was 1:00 in the night. I went to my room after the house lights went out, then I turned off my waist lights because I was used to sleeping in the dark. I didn't even know when I fell into a deep sleep.

That night was my worst night. I had a terrible dream that night.

I was wandering here and there in a forest. That forest was terrible. All kinds of sounds were coming, there were tall trees. I tried a lot to get out of that forest but failed. At last I saw a way out of him. In that forest I saw a lane which was a small and very narrow lane. In that street, I wandered here and there, I tried very hard to get out of that forest but then suddenly my eyes opened. For a while I did not understand where I was. Then I remembered that I was wandering in that forest but suddenly where did I come to my room?

Slowly the mind calmed down and then understood that it was a terrible dream. Actually I have nothing to do with that dream, but it was not so, I still feel that that dream is related to some point of my life. I had not only seen this dream that night, but I have seen this dream many times. The same forest, the same streets still come in my dreams, but maybe I have become used to it.

2. Zaira Ali

INTEZAAR

Love -just a four letter word but having power of overturning the world .

If it happens to you , it would blossom your heart and take you to the moon .

Or desert you as hell .

Yhhhh.....this is what love do .

With love , life too play games with us .It is as unexpected as love ,you don't know what would happen to you the very next moment.

Amazingly, this had happened to me . It was going all right .We were together for completely one year. Today we had our first anniversary .

But as life rule with every good news , a bad one come out with bonus.

Here is poem on this day from my memory treasure .

Wo din kch haseen tha

Syd jo hmare milne k dn tha

Charo trf jaise

Rango ki barsaat thi

Suraj bhi aj baadlo sang

Athkeliye kr rhe the

Main uski di hui

Lal libaz phne

Palke bichae uski yaadon me dubi thi

Saamein bhi madhosh ho rhi thi

Mil kr dhero bat krna

uske seene lg jane ki khwahish

Bs sir chd rhi thi

Ar zindagi ne karwat bdli

Intezar lambi hoti gyi

Saamein dhalne lgi

Har khawaish kaali hoti raatone me smaan lgi Meri hr uthti baithi dharkan ke

Saath waadon ki lari tutti gyi

Wo srf mera h k bhrm us roz jo tuta Meri Zindagi k khusiyun se nata tut gya . Ar isi trh hmara sath chutt gya.

Project Head's Desk

3. Krishna K. Bagdi

• • •

BE A WARRIOR, NOT A WORRIER

Everything comes in time to him who knows how to wait.

But if you can't wait you can't get the things you want in your life.

Success is not final, failure is not fatal: it is the courage to continue that counts.

Continue Doing

Of small works and dicision

One day make it Big story of your success. Never thought that you can't do it.

Make a list of your dreams

And set small goals and achieve your dreams.

No-one comes to support you.

At your struggle time.

When you get your dreams

And success

Every one came and say congratulations.

Strive not to be a success, but rather to be of value.

Pain is temporary.

Quitting lasts forever.

HardWork pain is temporary

Regret pain is permanent.

Co-author's Desk

4. Har Deepansh Bahadur Sinha

He is Har Deepansh Bahadur Sinha. He belongs to Lucknow,UP. He isa research scholar of Oceanography and has done masters in Geography from National Post Graduate College. Completed his schooling from Study Hall.His hobbies are art , listening to music cooking & loads of driving. His interest areas are Astronomy,Writing,Photography & Travelling a lot. You can contact him on Instagram @Deepansh_sinha

BELOVED NIGHT TALES

Those were the best moments Which enhanced our excitment, Eagerly waited for the night To board on fairytales flight. The pilot was none other Than my own grandmother, Begin with the story of a child Who was notorious and wild. Next in the box was fairies Fascinating was their stories, Panchtantra was also entertaining All the characters were captivating. All brothers were story lover For stories disturbed our mothers, Some of them were so terrifying A calm night turned into horrifying. Genuinely we forgot our chapters Champak was full of laughters, Slowly slowly night tales went far Still we remember without any scares. A heartiest thanks to grandparents Those stories were not less than presents, Also a thankyou to our beloved parents For completing the missing segments.

UNFORGETTABLE TRIP

I didn't thought for a power nap Once I got lost In nature's lap, All around there was fascinating greenery I didn't miss a single captivating scenery. Hill stations have got unique qualities They are full of hidden specialities, Rivers flowing down will give you immense pleasure Genuinely the trip was completely full of treasures. That place was just beyond imagination Till date it's my favorite destination, Every location has got wonderful vibes The feeling that words cannot describe. When somebody talks about marvelous place I get nostalgic with tremendous grace, I can't survive without exploring That's why I love traveling.

5. Mohammed Niyaz

Mohammed Niyaz hails from Mumbai - The City Of Dreams. He often loves to write poetries and short music video stories for his own youtube channel. Apart from this Mohammed is currently working on his upcoming anthologies, as well writing poetries since 2013. You can nd him on facebook/mohammed niyaz as well on instagram @niyazsks.

LOVE OF LIFE

She took the opportunity to give us birth. With whatever she can lead up til worth. Her nature gave me what I never asked. Several happiness till countless booked. The initiative to train the time was perfect. In the proper situation of effect. Her arms led my wings fly. Top above the seven heavens of sky. Success stood beside me furthermore appreciation. Backing back to back fame of mention. The more the merrier became house of hour. Leading to timingly presentation of our.

We can't afford her efforts of rife. Been a memorable "love of life".

6. Muralidhar Bansal

He is Muralidhar Bansal from Nepal. He loves writing as a hobby and started writing when he was a student, having seen the environmental around him. You can contact him on Instagram @writings_from_heart_92

MEMORIES

It is said no one moves for long in life. But memories do walk for long and help in regaining moments.

Memories are hidden. But its visibility can be felt in the loneliness.

Memory can't be felt by those who erase it, but it can be felt by those who live in it's moments.

No matter to what extent we try to forget the bygone days, but these are still hovering around us; perhaps to gather some new way of living.

Memories can't be forgotten by forgetting. These come and go like the shadow in the brightness.

Not all memories gain momentum. Some are forgettable, some are kept for great moments while some of these remain in heart for eternal.

Memory is that seed of a plant which when watered with courage of moving ahead can bring the fruitful moments in future.

Memories ate also strange at times, we often memorize those moments in life which are rather rude and nightmares.

7. Shubhanjali Nishad

She is Shubhanjali Nishad from Kanpur (Uttar Pradesh). She is completed graduation. Writing is her passion. Her hobbies are dancing, reading and writing. Contact her on Instagram @Painfull_lafz13

❧❧❧

YAADON KE KHAZANE

Yaadon k khazane se chalo kuch pal chura lete hai

Kuch lamhe jo yadein bn gyi hai chlo aj un palon ko Firse jeene ja luft utha lete hau

Chlo yaadon k kahazano se kuch pal chura lete hai

Kuch khatti kuch meethi yaadon ko ek mothi mein piro k un yaadon ki ladiyo ko mala bma lete hai

Koun jane kitna waqt hai kisk paas jindagi jeene ka hai

Chlo jn hassen yaadon k khazane bhare pal r se jeek apno k saath thoda waqt gujar lete hai

Bahut chotti c jindagi hai kb tham jaye sansei Koun jane chlo yaadon k sahare bichde hue logo ko

Yaad krk apni jindagi k kuch pal hasee khushi se beeta lete hai.

Yaadon k khazano ka mol koi na jane jb log bichad jate hai

Tab yaadon k sahare jindagi k kuch pal nikl jate hai

Log mit jate hai mitti ki tarah kuch haseen pal bikhar jate hai ban k rait ki tarah

Tb wo yaadon ka khazana hi kaam aata hai Tbhi apno k jane k baad unka ehsaas is haadd tk

Dil ko jhakjhor jata hai Insan toh jinda reh jata hai pr mare saman hojata hai
Unn toh jindagi jinda lash bn kaat nahi sakte
Apno ko jinda rkhne k liye unki muskan ko waps lane k liye ek yahi yaadon ka khazana hi bachta hai
Jo mare hue insan ko jeene ki wajh seekha jata hai.

8. Noor Tabassum

The name of the author is Noor Tabassum. Writing is her passion. She is an author in Scribe Mag magazine and a blogger in Times of India. She is also a regular poet in Muse India- my space. She has participated in more than 250 anthologies. She has also written solo books called 'Sensibles' and 'Twisted Firsts'. She is a nature lover and loves to lead a simple life. She expresses all her feelings in her writing as she thinks it is the most powerful medium to communicate. Her thoughts and writings are appreciated a lot and she has won many competitions even. You can contact her on Instagram @noortabassumali123

MEMORIES

Swaying on the swings, climbing trees, and sprinting, No anxiety of the world nor any obligations haunting,
An entire day playing with friends, arguing, and brawling,
The very next instant, again cuddling and giggling.
I never thought these days of childhood would fade so soon,
Granny's stories slowly were ignored in the afternoon, I never realized when I grew out of the cocoon, And escalated into a buttery trying to reach the moon. Spent countless nights in the cozy arms of the beloved, Under the sky, staring at the impish stars, drowned,
His chest was my pillow, and his arms as blanket covered,
But these days also sailed away, leaving me alone and depressed.
Now I am left with nothing but memories,

Eyes flood when they pass by me, intensifying my worries,

Putting a sweet smile on my face as they are my only treasuries.

And time slips from my hand as if it is in a hurry.

HAUNTING MEMORIES OF THE PAST

Today, as I sat sipping my coffee, drowning in loneliness,

My sight got caught at an album at the far end lying in quietness,

I approached to have a glance at it and recall all my naughtiness,

And I was lost in a world of wonder which I once lived with happiness.

Those days when I an apple of the eye of my parents,

The days when I troubled them for so many toys, and they ran errands,

The days I was pampered like a princess and dressed like a rabbit,

To click pictures and to play with was their habit. The days when friends roamed without fear,

Met my sweetheart who had given my owers as memoirs,

Where have those days gone when we lived life with full zeal,

Today all are roaming in the empty lanes of memories, and life seems like a jail.

9. Avani Jain

Avani is a thoughtful and sensitive teen writer and poet. She writes about what she has witnessed or learnt from life.She pours her heart out in her writings. To her , poetry is a place where she can let her emotions out without any fear. When her pen and paper meet amazing creations are born.

MEMORY LANE

Memories are indeed a timeless treasure of the heart Once you open this treasure

You can't just do with a single part

Whether it's just a mere flashback or a picture of your childhood art

The single part unleashes a chain of many more

It might also be the sound of waves you heard by the shore

It's true that you'll relive a bunch of moments more When I walk past this memory lane

I recall all the tears of joy and gloom that I did gain.

10. Rachana Saha

Rachana Saha, a budding writer. She has a great interest and love in writing. She bleeds her feelings in her diary. She is in class 8 reading in St. Xavier's Institution. She is born and brought up in Kolkata. She is co-author of many anthologies and wants to write more. She is compiler of two books THE BLANK PAGE and BLEEDING METAPHOR. Other than writings, she has a great interest in drawing. You can contact her on Instagram @r.a.c.h.a.n.a.s.a.h.a.

AN ODE TO THE UNBORN CHILD TO THE MOTHER
Maa, don't let me go,
I want to see the world
And know what you know.
I want to see the world,
How people are good,
How it was few days back.
They say you have to leave me,
They say you are unlucky,
They say you were yonderly everytime.
The breeze was rude,
The flower didn't bloomed,
It died under longing days
But who cares?
The loss was a tribute
To the seeds to be sown.

I can't say my word,

I kick you everyday,

But maa, one day I felt

I was vanishing and

Going miles apart.

Someone was pulling me,

Out of your body, "Aaah"

"Aah" you screamed, you cried.

Everyone was in hurry.

The doctor asked, "either maa or child" Papa was numb,

Granny decide to save you, mumma, For she could never see me alone,

The world so cruel

Maa you were never selfish,

It was maybe me who didn't have luck To see the world, for once.

I don't want to see the world,

Without you,

Don't want to know what you know, I knew what you believe.

I couldn't wipe your tears,

But could feel it.

Maa, my those little part

Are dead now.

You cried,

I believed.

I died,

You became heartless.

11. Javeria Saghir

"No doubt, passion comes before talent." Javeria Saghir from Lahore, Pakistan - is pursuing graduation in the eld of chemistry from GCUF. Apart from study, she has a keen interest in creative writing, poetry, singing, and artwork. She began writing in 2020 and achieved several certicates and positions in online writing competitions. She is adaptive and a passionate dreamer who has a firm belief that consistency and hard work will enable her to attain the impossible and make her strong enough to sparkle the lives of others. You can contact her on Instagram @passionforart_02

ACROSTIC POEM- MEMORIES

M: Moments apparently etched in mind,

E: Embracing instants of different times,

M: Making unintentionally sink in thoughts lined,

O: Often ooding backward aligned,

R: Revisiting the special glimpses shined,

I: In that frame of time, unforgettable signed,

E: Even if it becomes past that one, can't find,

S: Silently surrender one, make the thoughts tined.

12. Srija Sadhukhan

Srija Sadhukhan is 19 years old girl studying BSc Biotechnology in Amity University Kolkata. Love to write poetry and a book worm too. You can contact her on Instagram @syncopatemysuccess

MEMORIES OF LOVE AND DESIRE
As I sit and wonder
How much important in my life you are?
The way you hold me tight in your arm
I can still feel that charm.
When you are with me,
I never felt lonely And our love
Words reside in each other's heart quietly.
Each qnd everytime when
I talk to you I discover something
Delightful and new,
Our love seems perfect.
I want to sit beside you
Enjoying the shining star
And blue view,
The tides blow apart
And my calm beating heart
The melodies I often croon.
Promised not to leave each other hand
To dive into the love land,

When you are not with me
An emptiness evolves me,
My life looks dull with you.
I love the way You add stability
And desire in my life everyday,
I want to stay with you like this my dear
Forever happy and mear
To fulll our love and desire.
I don't know how to express
But I have a lot of feelings to confess,
How your voice gives me butteries
And when you stare at me with those loveable eyes,
To stay together forever.

13. Harshita Verma

Co-author Harshita Verma is a writer from Lucknow. She has completed her graduation in commerce stream. She has been writing poetry for the last few years as her passion. She wants to be a novelist in future. You can contact her on Instagram @0_hsh

MEMORIES OF SCHOOL DAYS
Walking past the school today
I realised how much
I missed those days.
The days where every moment was joyful
The moment when you sat for your boards
Nervous but writing with great condence.
The moment when you became the captain
Proud and excited for the coming journey.
The days where every single minute
With friends turned into true friendship.
The moment when you first entered the school
Afraid but ready to learn something new.
The moment when you said goodbye to school in farewell
Upset but ready for a new life.
School where every moment taught something
Which cannot be ever forgotten.

MEMORIES

Reminding of the good days
Reminding of the hard days
Memories are like a ride of life
Some fair some bad but a part of life.
Easier to create but harder to forget
The moments captured in the mind
The creator of a person's identity
Memories a part of our entity
Reminder of how old days went
Sometimes teaching sometimes not
But always special for the heart
Such are the memories of life
Remembering them when mind feels
Missing them hoping to bring them back
Those days spent happily are now memories.

14. Dreamer

Dreamer is writer by passion. Trying to pen down certain episodes and trying to relive them vicariously through reader's word of praise.

For more of Dreamer's scenic nazams, you can visit Instagarm profile : vicissitudeing_prespective

BHULIBISRI YAADEIN

Yaad hai wo din..

Jab tumhe tumhari har baat mujhe baatne ki bechaini rehti thi..,

Meri har baat jab tumse shuru hi hoti thi..,

Tumhari aankho me jab sab mera naam padhne lage the..,

Kisi ki nigaho ko jab sirf tumhara hi intezaar rehto tha..,

Appki har adaa hum par kuch aanoka jadu kar jati thi..,

Tumne aapne aap par haaq de diya tha bin kuch kahe..,

Aur humne aapki hasi, aapke aasu, aapki har taklif ko appna maan liya tha.. . .

Aaj yaado ka pitara khola to ye kuch purane panne bhi nikal aae unn bhulibisri yaado ke..

TMHARE INTEZAARR MEIN

Wo bhi kya din the, jab..

Haazaro ki bheed me tanha se rehte the,

tere intezar me..

Tere saath bitane ko kuch lamhe,

Bita diye karte the humn kai aarse bas tere khayalo me..

Jab tum aae nahi milne humse,

Ye keh kar k mashroof the tum,

'Kabhi aur sahi' : soch kar,

Nadan sa ye dil ek aarsa guzarne ki thaan leta tha,

Sirf tumhare intezar me...!!!

15. Aanushnaa Bandyopadhyay

Aanushnaa Bandyopadhyay is a girl from Kolkata, studying in St. Xavier's Institution, class 8. She loves showing her creativity through arts and wants to be a professional violinist and a great writer. She's currently the Brand ambassador of a Reputed Publication and the Founder of Inking Hearts Writing Community. She has worked as the compiler of three books, namely, "The Independent Pen", "The Saga of Love" and "Women, not Weak", among which two came in the top 100 bestselling books on Amazon. She had also been a co-author of 90+ anthologies and won many writing challenges held by various writing communities. You can contact her on instagram- @bandyopadhyay.aanushnaa_2020

SCHOOL BUS CAME

It was 10 AM in the morning, he woke up with his mother's high pitched voice asking him to wake up. Sitting up in bed, he yawned casually, as he knew online classes don't need anything other than joining the meeting and keeping video and mic off... Suddenly, her mother called out, " Get ready quickly, your school bus will be coming soon! " He got a slight heart attack. After a pause of few minutes, he shouted, " Which school bus? Why? When? " Her mother replied, " I told you last night that I received a message from your school about reopening of your school. You told that it was okay, so I didn't disturbed you again! " " Mamma, I had my headphones on, I wasn't able to heard you...! "complained the boy. " I don't know what you'll

do, just pack your bag and get ready, you have ten minutes time. "
He rushed for washroom. Today, he took only 1 minute to brush and
bath, unlike other days when he usually took 1 hour time for the
same. He then ran to his study table to nd his books and bag, but
it wasn't there. He searched his whole room, and at last he found his
bag from his shoecase. Packing his books, he went searching for his
uniform, which was found in his almirah after a search of nearly 5
mins. At last, he got ready. He tied his shoes and was ready to left
for the school bus, when his mother came to him and told, " Good
morning, Dear! I guess...you're waiting for the bus, so sorry, I lied to
you! I just wantedyou to revive your old routine again. " said she with a
guilty tone. Though he felt relieved hearing that the school isn't open,
he felt sad at that same time, remembering his school. The memories
of getting up early and prepare for school, the memories of meeting
friends on the school bus, and other precious moments that he spent at
the school. Though, he was scared after hearing the reopen of school,
but he was heartbroken to return back after getting ready for school..

16. Rimjhim Agrawal

Her name is Rimjhim Agrawal and she was born on 16 April 2003. She lives in Gorakhpur UP and she loves helping others as when she wanted support she have no one so she knows the pain and her quotes r just a way of expressing her feelings as she has written 30 + anthologies book and she loves singing ,dancing, cooking , comedy etc.You can contact her on Insrtagram @Rimjhimagrawal409 .

BROKEN HEART

Every moment of my eyes reminds me of you
The way you hold my hand besides every
Harmful people's reviews
I still remember you saying
I love you Whenever i missed you
I know we are over but still the part of me
Knows you are here for me just to make
Sure I am happy with my own ?,
No commitments no relationship but
I want to still tell you that
I love you just the way you do ?

NIGHTMARE

It's feels like I am living in my dreams ?
And you are holding my hand full night

Just to talk with me?you are suffering
From this stupid fu**ing society rights ?
As Loving me is the only motive of your life
Just to tell you I also love you
Still the moon and lovely sunrise

17. Ishika Jha

Step down into your heart and let the ink drip the magic is what the writer Ishika believes in, a 17 year old girl who wishes to pen down all her emotions behind words of poetries to escape from the fake world around her and spread love and hope amongst every individual reading her writeups. Along with music and sketching, writing is her passion which she's currently working on through different writing platforms. You can contact her on Instagram @ishika_0125

DESTINED US

Memories of us being together
Memories of us being for each other,
Are just some random thoughts striking
My mind at the midnight hour,
I know we aren't meant to be,
But i really wish we could,
Atleast then these memories wouldn't be the one,
I would be living with,
On seeing our old photographs,
These memories are the ones that cones
Knocking at the door of my heart,
And doesn't let the comfort go in vein....
My best memory to recall,
Is the gift of your presence.

18. E M Devi Shree

She is a passionate writer. She's doing her bachelor's degree in Physics Research. She's a social activist and talks on social issues.

Instagram:- @_thelunar_writer_._

BRING BACK MY DAYS

To sit on the roof top,

With tears in eyes,

Heavy memories in heart,

His promises in my thoughts,

Lost pain, Lost him......

Eyes sleep, Memories won't!

Bring back my memories,

Bring back my Lost life,

Bring back some Previous days,

Where I laughed, And Now I cry!

19. K.Eswari

Miss K.Eswari from virudhunagar. Completed Bachelor of Arts (B.A.English) at V.V.Vannia perumal college virudhunagar and doing Bachelor of Education (B.Ed) in Srividya college of Education under (TNTEU). Awsome motivational speaker.Great optimistic person.co author for nearly 80 anthologies (both tamil and english). One of The awarde in blue star awards.Her way of describing words are very much optimistic.It is her poem. Hope you like her poem. Love her writings very much.In addition,she is interested in drawing. A nice singer and a awsome cook. She is one of my best inspiration.A good supporter. Hope she become a great realistic writer in future. A simple girl with lots of dream. Miss K.Eswari from virudhunagar. Completed Bachelor of Arts (B.A.English) at V.V.Vannia perumal college virudhunagar and doing Bachelor of Education (B.Ed) in Srividya college of Education under (TNTEU). My best inspiration.A good supporter. Hope she become a great realistic writer in future. A simple girl with lots of dream. Connect her on Instagram @eswarikumaran2311

BROTHER'S LOVE

The awesome king of my world!

The second father!

The another mother!

The best motivator!

The awsome inspiration!

The treasure box of happiness!

The awsome saint of virtues!

The awsome lover of my naughtiness!

The best crime partner!

The best critic!

The soul of sacristy1!

The dreamer of my success!

The warrior against my worries!

The awesome commander of my life!

The great killer of my worries!

The awsome medicine for all my pains,

The immortal candle of love!

The awesome pretector!

The best solution for all my problems!

I am nothing without you!!

20. Muskan Kesarwani

This muskan Kesarwani is a resident of Prayagraj Katghar, She has just completed her post graduation, she is fond of writing and she wants to go further in this line, she has participated in many anthology so far, now she is writing her own book. Wants to have full cooperation of all the friends of their family in this journey, their brothers encourage them for every good work and we wish that they get a lot of progress in this, she is also a teacher and writer by profession, she is the author complire also working as. You can contact her on Instagram @heartless_mussu

MUJHE BHULAE NAHI BHULTE WO PAL

Muje bhulaye nahi bhulte wo pal

Jis waqt hum dono mile the kal

Tum jo hath chuda ke ja rhe the kal

Jaan meri ja rhi thi pal pal

Tumne to asani se kh diya tha kal

Tum mere nahi ho ab

Tumne ek baar bhi socha tha kya biti hogi mujpe us waqt

Til til toot chuki thi mai usi waqt

Muje wo pal bhulaye nahi bhul rahe

Jis waqt tumne hath choda tha mera kal

Meri lahjti aakhe bhi na tum pachan paye kal

Jinhe dekh k kabhi tum likhte the gajal

Kisi gair ke liye choda hai muje to

Ye bhi bata do usse bhi chodoge kab tk

Laut ke aane ki bhul bhi mat karna ab

Tumre liye khatm ho chuke hai wo

Jajbat jo mere dil me the tumahre liye kal tak.

UNFORGETTABLE MEMORIES

Bade shauk se mohabat kiya tha na tumne bhi or humne bhi to tumhari yaad sirf muje hi kyu aaati hai

Do aakhe to kudrat ne tumhe bhi diye hai to ye yaade tumhe kyu nahi rualati hai

Raato ke kale ghanee andhere me meri bhi yaade tumhe kyu nahi tadpati hai

Bade shauk se mohabat kiya tha na tumne bhi or humne bhi to tumhari yaad sirf muje hi kyu aaati hai

Hath thama tha na tumne to kyu chod diya kya meri

Masoom si akho ko rota dekh tumko daya jara bhi na aati hai

Najre milte hi churane lagte ho aakhe

Aapni lagta hai gairo ki bahon me haya tumhe bhi thodi aati hai

Aacha ye batao kya din ke ujjalo me

Khawabo khaylo me meri yaad tumko jara si bhi satati hai

Bade shauk se mohabat kiya tha na tumne bhi or humne bhi to tumhari yaad sirf muje hi kyu aaati hai.

21. Varsha Sahu

Varsha Sahu is a beginner under the roof of literature. seek new creation.she loves to entwine her ideas in word to present a poetic picture. her passion for throughs and words is breathing through her poetry. she can write in both languages hindi and english. she is a book worm and she loves traveling and interacting with new people. she belongs to chhattisgarh M.P.

MEMORY
Even the nights brought you memory,
Even the rains brought your memory,
The evening brought you memory,
The moon brought your memory,
Brought you memory,
Together of two couples,
Some songs brought to your memory,
Missed you when i laughed,
Missed you when i cried.

22. Saniya Varghese

Saniya Varghese is a 13 year old girl who loves to overthink. She loves superstitional characters.Most of the works of hers are full of her imagination which leads the reader to an amazing imaginary world and she's a published co -author of more than 20 book and compiler of 3 . She prefer's to be alone, in an imaginary world. Instagram id : _saniya_varghese_

AMOUR

I was just a broken piece of glass,
Not until I met you,
You made me complete!
Without you, I can't even think of a day living.
I was just a breathing soulless body
Which you made come to life
I donno what could have been to me,
If you were never with me
You were just one among those strangers
Whom I never even glanced
But now you made me fall head over toes for you
Within this time you made a irreplaceable place
For yourself in my heart
You took what was left of my heart
You became my everything,
Which I never wished for

But can't deny that I can't live without you,
Even a day now.

23. Aiwa Antonya

Aiwa Antonya a simple teenager. Who's lost in a world of art a silent writer. She loves to sing as well. No matter where ever she is a diary and pen will be always with her. Her Instagram Id is @aiwa.oncover

SHE'S STILL ALIVE

I'm a writer who loves to spend time in solitude That was not the case But after the death of my dear friend, everything seemed to be falling apart ...

Something was missing from me wandering in that sea of grief

It took me a while to figure out what it was .. Yes! I'm lost myself ... that's what's hard to get back

She was very dear to me

Maybe a good sister above all ...

One day she was removed from this world by giving me so many good and sad memories to remember Without even giving me a hint ... why did she leave without even keeping her words to me?

To this day I am still unable to find answers to these questions

Maybe there is no answer?

I dont know that either

I miss going to the Riverside with her

We usually spent hours there after school..

Sitting together in a bench

Writing something or singing together...

Today when i remember about the normal things that happened between us..

Tears from my eyes flow down the cheeks

I do not want to write about her but everything I write is only about her

And sometimes it makes me think a lot

early morning. today i decided to go to the river side ...

Maybe it's because of the desire to experience those emotions again ...

I haven't came here ever since her death

The river is as calm as ever

Her seat on the bench where we used to sit together is empty

I know she won't come .. but why am I waiting?

I enjoyed the beauty of the calm river

All the old memories were remembered

I cried a lot today than usual

There was a downside to her absence

I can't see anyone else in her position ..

One day I will have to say goodbye to this world Before that I have a lot things to complete

Who knows if I'll die flashing in my head

The very next moment

I started walking on the way to Home Looking at the sky..

I know somewhere there

She's watching me

And here in my heart she's still alive.

24. Juliet Hudait

Juliet Hudait is a 15 year old who's passionate about Photography, Music and Writing. She is a Bibliophile and an Astrophile. She has co-authored 115 books and she's currently compiling 7 books. Connect with her on Instagram @juliethudait

A LETTER TO MY LOVE

To,

Alex….

Hey love! Hope you're doing fine. I wanted to write this letter to you asking you to hold my hand forever no matter what happens. Whatever be the obstacles in our path, never leave me no matter what. The day I first met you as a casual tuition senior is the one I'm going to remember forever. I never thought I would actually fall in love with you. The day we sat and watched a video together about time travelling, was the first time we were so close to each other. It was such an amazing day. Unfortunately I had to break from tuition then because I wanted to study on my own. Instagram bought us together again in the month of April. That one story reply you sent me was the start of it all. Though you never told me directly, I got to know what you felt for me and I behaved rude with you since I never wanted to get into any relationship. I want to thank you for bearing all of that and being there for me though I hurt you. I realised your love for me with time and I accepted you in the month of August which was probably the happiest moment for both of us.

Since August we have had a lot of fights and a lot of good times too. You've stayed up late night just to talk to me because I felt low, you chat with me even though you're busy and you meet me with so much risk whenever I miss you. I never wanna lose someone like you since you always care about me more than your ego. In every fight, you're the first one to apologise even though you have no fault and all of this shows how much you love me and that you never want to lose me. Most important of all: you've changed my personality! You've changed the person I was in the past. You taught me how to love and care. You taught me that love is more important than ego. You helped me by asking me to share all of my problems and I'm grateful to have someone like you in my life.

I never wanna lose you my love! Hold my hand forever......

From,

Juliet

25. Mohammed Sohail

He is Mohammed Sohail from Hyderabad. Pusuing Bsc. Nutrition. He loves to explore himself more and more through his pen. He also took a part in many anthologies.You can contact him on Instagram @Sohail_quotes22

YAADON KA BAQSA

Kaha gaya wo yaadon ka baaksa

Jismein sara bachpan sama beta tha

Wo jab dheku

Wo sara bachpan samne dikhta tha

Zindagi ke udaan tho udli humein

Aabh wo bachpaan kaha tha

Wo din bhi tho yaadon ka baksa bangayi thi.

LOVE WITH MY ANGEL

Zindagi guzaar gaayi thi

Uske yaadon mein laafz jo chup gaya

Hooton ke chaadar mein

Liptha hua tha tera badan

Mere bahaon mein

Kuch yaadein thi taaaza

Bankar kar reh gayi uska baksein mein

Lautna tha aapein ghaar

Tere yaadon mein
Jo tu zindgi ke chadaar ko chod gayi thi

26. Mohd Faisal Khan

Name- Mohd Faisal Khan

Education- He has done his SSC and SSSC completed from Kendriya vidyalaya Cantt Faizabad with first division.

Graduation done from Aligarh Muslim University in B.A (Hons) political science with first division.

Post graduation done from Aligarh Muslim University in MBA (Agribusiness) with first division (Gold medalist).

Hobbies- writing, Travelling, playing, singing and reading.

He is singing a song and playing games from childhood and he writed his first poetry in 2011.

He has a good player and Participated in sports meet at school (regional level) and College level in table tennis and got first position.

He has also Participated in extra calicular activities like singing, self composed poetry and naat khawani at University level in Aligarh Muslim University and winning many prizes and certificates.

He love to spend his time in critical thinking and writing with strong positive attitude.

He love to implement his theoretical knowledge into practical work.

He also love to hear each and everyone to learn new

thinking and knowledge.
He love to read the writer and poet as well.

YAAD AATA HAI

Kabhi koi aaena koi chehra yaad aata hai,
Maazi ka guzra waqt ab bhot yaad aata hai.

Shab hote hi andheri raton me sitaro ke saath,
Kisi ko apne hathon pe sulana yaad aata hai.

Agar takleef dard gham naa aae paas,
To kaha kisi ko yaha khuda yaad aata hai.

Zinda hun kaise, ab mujhe ye hairat hoti hai,
Har baat pe kasam khana tera yaad aata hai.

Tumhe apne gunaho ka darr tak nahi hota,
Mujhe apni saans pe maut ka farishta yaad aata hai.

Tum hi the tumhara saaya tha yaa koi aur tha,
Tumahre saath guzara ek ek pal yaad aata hai.

Tum hi nahi yaha koi bhi ek kadam naa chal saka,
Sabka milna bichhadna bhot yaad aata hai.

Ab dekhte hai ansu apni ankho me jab "Faisal",
Hasi ka wo zamana tab bhot yaad aata hai.

27. Rajashree Bhuyan

Dynamic, bright and charismatic, Rajashree Bhuyan
born in the year 2002 in Jorhat,Assam has been awarded
with the Aspirant Achievers Dr. A.P.J Abdul Kalam
Award in 2021.She has completed her schooling from
Royal Oak High School , Jorhat , Assam and her higher
education from Pragya Academy , Jorhat . She is a
Bachelor of Science student now in Chemistry.
Morever , She is a journalist, speaker, author ,compiler
of three anthologies, project head and co- author in many
anthologies. Connect her on Instsagram
@Rajashree2700

CHILDHOOD SWEET MEMORIES
Childhood the best part of life
No problem no tension
Happy those early days! when
I Shined in my angel infancy.
Before I understood this place
Appointed for my second race,
Or taught my soul to fancy aught
But a white, celestial thought;
When yet I had not walked above
A mile or two from my rst love,
And looking back, at that short space,

Could see a glimpse of His bright face;
When on some gilded cloud or ower
My gazing soul would dwell an hour,
And in those weaker glories spy
Some shadows of eternity

28. Tahreem Afzal

Her name is Tahreem Afzal. She has done her MS in Mathematics. She is the author of "My Soul's Cravings" published by Daastan Publication. She has also worked as Co-author in many anthologies, and currently compiling her own one too. Besides being a dream hunter, she is the girl who is traveling on the path called 'life'. She doesn't complain for the obstacles, she just makes sure that her faith never gets blurry, as this is the only candle of light which keeps her going in dark nights. Connect her on Instagram @Reemsays789

LIVING IN MEMORIES

The people who once said that they would die without you,
Ask them why they are still alive although you left.
Not everyone can understand what love actually needs.
It needs whole of you, it needs your sensible promises
Which you can later fulll, and it needs you to understand
That dying is easy for someone,
living a life in someone's memories is what really love
is.

THOSE GOODBYES

Goodbyes are always hard for me; more like impossible. It is not because I don't know how to wave back at someone who has already did. It is not because I don't know how to say "Bye" to someone who is all ready to leave. It is just that I couldn't learn how to chain my tears for the person with whom I had imagined my whole life. I still don't know how to manage myself with the memories that will haunt my broken dreams, and moments in which I will miss the presence of the person for whom I got addicted.

29. Hema Kirthiga J

She is Hema Kirthiga J, and her pen name is Hyson. She is professionally a psychologist and passionately a writer. She heals others but writing heals her. She is writer, reader, orator and a believer. She is from Chennai. She lives by the principal of inspire and be inspired. She writes her heart and soul and she deeply believes that the depth of her heart and the nib of her pen are soulfully connected. Writing is an art and she is a proud artist. She loves what she does and loves what she writes. You can reach her at Instagram- @the_pen_queen Yourquote –JKM

WALKING ON THE MEMORY LANE
Those childhood lled with sweetness,
I hold those fond memories close!
Little child wandering around with no care about the world!
Love being showered all around!
Being appreciated for whatever you do!
I learned happiness there!
Acceptance abd appreciation came,
Even when I was not aware!
But, they are like dreams!
That the adult me is trying to Achieve,

And I don't know why it's so hard!
At least I could live on those memories.

30. Yasir Ali Durrani

His name is Yasir Ali Durrani.He is Currently Doing his Doctor Of Pharmacy.He has worked as Coauthor in many Anthologies and does writing especially Poetry as a passion without the greed of any money.He writes because he loves to write and whenever he feels to write.He loves to embrace and overcome challenges of life and that's what makes him special because it widens up his view of seeing the world and keeps him for to think of. Insta: @mysterical_oaths

FEEL YOU

Sat beneath an old willow tree
No enough energy to
Even raise my fallen head
Like a dead ower
That froze from misery
That wilted through the misery
And then nally died
But whether died
At peace or at chaos
Too dead to even
Look up at the moon
Or at the stars and
Bleed my heart out

Just by looking at them.

SWEET OR BITTER

Sweet in her own way
Bitter in her own
Sweet to show love
Sweet when beneath
The full moon listening
To my heart murmurs
Bitter to show love
Bitter to protect me
Bitter to prevent the scars
That tear my heart out
Sweet or Bitter?!
Maybe both yet still
Mine and for me.

31. Soniya Varghese

Soniya Varghese is a writer lled with her own euphoria.
She is a person who remains euphoric to see the kindred
and emotions evoked around her. She is an author who
handles mostly romantic themes and fun thrillers which
is both for teens and adults. Especially anyone who have
once fallen in love in their life. Whenever she writes she
takes a part from her own life. Her writings reects all that
she had experienced in her life. Anyone who reads all
her writings can connect it with her life. Instagram:
soniya__ varghese, Facebook: Soniya Varghese, Twitter:
@SoniyaVarghese8

THE WAY TURNED INTO A MEMORY
I miss the sun Memories are keeping me alive in this
eternal life of mine.
The life which I'm having now was never meant to be
mine.
It's just that somehow I ended up having a life of
eternity.
It seems like yesterday but it's already been a 100 years
till I've been to the sunlight.
I'm no longer a human. I'm turned into a vampire.
Someone who can no longer get exposed to sunlight.

The only thing I miss in this eternal life is me being in
sunlight.
Why did I ended up like this?
I've been to almost every corner if this world till now but
what can I do.
I can do nothing but just running away from sun the
thing which I loved the most.
The memories are still kept in me like a treasure.
If I didn't had these memories of being a human.
I'd have ended up killing everyone who came accross
me.
Thanks to my treasured memories giving me hope to live
long.

32. Priya Das

She is Priya Das, passionate about writing and paintings. She is a trained artist, calligrapher and a published writer. She loves to play with beautiful words and is fond of reading books.Her writings portray a contrast of nature and a glimpse of reality of life .At present she is pursuing Bsc in Biotechnology. Connect her on Instagram @the_poet_gallery

A MEMORABLE DAY WITH MY FRIEND

Today I open the diary of my life, Full with experience and memories of my life.Some are good,some are bad, still I am glad, I have all that - I have captured all in my heart, And my ink captured in my memorable diary. At that moment when I opened the doors of my diary I was overwhelmed with all my emotions . All the memories refresh my soul. But among all the pages I got stuck with the photo of my school trip which was the last trip and the end of my school life. It was the most memorable day of life . Me and my school friends went in a trip to visit North East India. I guess no place can be more captivating than the surrounding of nature. Wherever the eyes goes on Hills and Hills!! Greenery and blue sky all over, beautiful birds,tribes of diverse community, owers, waterfalls. Cant explain the beauty of nature in my words. The journey with your best friends hits differently, isn't it??? The path full of joy , songs, food, friends, nature and most importantly memories. What can be better than this??

NECTAR OF MY CHILDHOOD

Whenever the sweet wind blows it reminds me the
blissful memories of my childhood.
The glorious evenings of my life when me and my old
friends played under the velvet sky .
The chirping of birds and the roaming of cotton clouds in
the vast empyrean.
The jiggling of tree leaves and the bright flowers.
Ohh!! What a pleasant moment of my village life.
The soothing cool touch of wind maked it more magical
To feel the past memories of my childhood.
In the sunny summer the blissful wind had given a relief
To our energetic soul to live a life in our playful time.

33. Mahesh R

MAHESH by name 5.9 ft tall, a simple person easy going and honest. From chill city Hosur (little England mazzive) completed his P. G in govt arts and science college hosur. Nature lover intrested in writing, painting, mocking, loving and helping. You can contact him on Instagram @Call_me_Happiness

NOT A DREAM

A month of august
The first little drop from a dark big cloud
Comes with sound of thunder a loud
It was an ordinary day
But it takes me in pleasant way
World full of flowers
A extreme lovable followers
Surprisingly i am invincible
And too invisible
But thoughts about my lady love
Still it reminds she is flying dove
Stop said to mind
Don't want to be hide
I want to forget and not be haunted
Let me feel your mesmerising charm
Take me agin in your harm....

34. Kashish Yadav

Her name is Kashish Yadav . She lives in Lucknow. She is studying. She had done a drama on ROMEO- JULIET play. She is passionate with her works. She is so hardworking girl. She is versatile. She loves to write her thoughts , poem and short stories. She daily write her thoughts on Your quote app. Her thoughts are available on Google by Kashish Yadav quotes . She had worked in so many anthologies and she got so many certicate for writing her thoughts on daily challenges. She is fond of listening to music and dancing. She wants to become an IAS officer. Connect her on Instagram @kashishyadav959

CHILDHOOD MEMORY

Used to search for the one who has childhood! You cheated X! You have trapped me in the trap of words All the streets have seen her too, her happiness is beautiful, dear, the memories of Pritam's songs are also lovely. Believe me, the life of my youth is very strange, aspirational effort, the heart of knowledge is captivating But this is the end, a heavy battleeld has become a world; in the midst of worry, life is also a burden. Come on, childhood! Once again, give your pure peace, the one who pacies the Every moment of life is very beautiful, but there is no time to feel it. I still remember my mother's lullaby, but no time to talk to my mother. To whom we work hard to give every happiness of life, but do not have time to give them. Remember all the childhood memories, but no time to remember them.

35. Sree Varshini R

Sree Varshini was born on 9th August 1996 in Kodaikanal . She loves to write poem and a short story since school days . she was participated in International paper presentation and won the best paper award. Her poem and short stories was published under around 70 anthologies .

WHEN I SAW MY KIDS SMILE
When I saw your smile for the first time
All my pains Gone through the miles
All my hurts vanish All my fears disappear
All my pain fades away
An unexpected arrival in the world
To make my life happy without untold
You don't know what you were doing
But I realized the extent of enjoying
Every time you were smiling unknowingly
But I felt its for me a big gift everyday
When I saw your smile for the first time
Like a rainbow , your smile appeared occasionally
But it made a bond unconditionally
Your smile is always innocent , my dear baby boy
Even when you are grown up as a guy.

WHEN MY DAY BECOMES MORE BEAUTIFUL

My day is more beautiful
When my schedule is wonderful
No hazard stress Nothing terrible
All prayerful wishes fullled
I am healthy and glad
Family and fantabulous friends
All in pink of health
Earning smart for wealth
Forever smile and live in mirth
The feel of the cool morning breeze
After an uninterrupted, sound sleep
A sip by sip of freshly brewed coffee in no hurry
With sumptuous breakfast to ll my tummy
A calm and peaceful ride to the workplace
In newly clad linen saree with grace
The sweet chorus of blushing, giggling buds
With friendly smile and greet of co-workers
A day well begun , gives us immense pleasure
That's to be cherished as a beautiful treasure.

36. Riya Richard R. L

Riya Richard R. L is a young, burgeoning writer in English. She has adored writing since her girlhood. She has a unique style and distinct modus operandi in her writings- poems, quotes, short stories, novels, etc... She has worked as a Co-author in 400+ anthologies. She is involved in Compiling and has Compiled three anthologies. Her first anthology published is 'Courage to Continue'.She is from Kanyakumari district, Tamil Nadu. She is now an undergraduate in Chemistry.Besides writing, she also loves reading books, drawing, arts and crafts, and learning. She is a lover of Nature.Connect her on Instagram @rl.riya21

THE TREASURE

The most unforgettable Memory in my Life is You,
That wonderful day, when For the first time,
I saw You, The day I froze on Seeing your Smile,
The day I lost myself On seeing your Eyes,
The day I fell in Deep Love with You,
The day I Met You,
The day I spoke with You,
The day I went out with You,
The day I spent with You,
The day I proposed to You,

The day I waited for your Answer,

It seemed like A thousand years,

I was worried But you made me Jump on Cloud Nine,

By Accepting me as your Life,

I couldn't forget that sweet Memories,

Which always remain In my Heart as The Treasure

37. Akash Singh

Akash Singh is the son of Mr.Anil Kumar Singh and Mrs.Sunita Singh.He is from Ghazipur,Uttar Pradesh but shifted to Varanasi due to academic reasons.He is the student of 12th Commerce from Udai Pratap Public School.He loves to write from October,2020.
Instagram:- @Anilsinghmahamantri

SISTER AND BROTHER

My best memory is with my sister cum bestie.
With her I play,eat,ght and love her
But it is the fact that most of the time we ght.
The day when we will not ght is something which no one can digest in our home.
And we can also not takes it good.
We will ght but this is the fact that we help each other,
Whenever we needed at that time we are like beasties for resties.
We both share everything either good or bad with each other
And it is the must we have a nick name for each other.
With all this ght and love we live together.
But the love matters as we have love in ght also.

FRIENDSHIP

My best memory is when I am a school boy, I met a girl looking very strange, Sitting alone in crowd and always thinking deeply, I think maybe she loves her own privacy, So I decided not to disturb her. But one day when she was sitting alone, I saw her crying And I decided now enough,I will ask from her as I don't have any more patience I get near to her and asked What happened to my lonely lover? She just hold my hands and crying and crying! I asked what happened at least tell me. And picks up the water bottle to give her water After than gives her my handkerchief. When she stopped crying I don't love privacy but in school no one want to be my friend! I replied who said this to you by laughing I am your friend and after that she smiled and asked my name! And that's how we became friends.

38. Sourishree Ghosh

Sourishree Ghosh is a 17 year old free-spirited soul from India. She is a co-author to different books . She is a Bharatanatyam dancer and painter . She believes writing to be a form of escapism.
Instagram:- @Srijonighosh961

TO THE LOVE I LOST
People say ," waiting is a sign of true love ",
And I waited forever for the reply of those unseen messages ,
To the affection I lost in waiting ,
People say ," silence is enough" .
I screamed in front of you ,not realised you were deaf and blind to love !
Isn't it strange that I went to the temple to pray for love?
People say ," everything comes at the right time ".
Some said yesterday," time will never be correct ".
Offine loves are true , online is something of an illusion ,
Maybe emojis don't say it all , Is interpreting someone correctly a sign of love
Or it's just a piece of common sense ,
For a person like me sitting on the last bench .
People say ," if you don't marry , for whom will you care for next ?"

I boast in blasted voice ," let me live for myself1!"

QUOTE- 1

I had to remember you as you were the one who came
with a wholesome smile , not a matter if without a gift .
My love doesn't have a shift .

QUOTE- 2

Meeting an unforgettable person after years is like nding
the centre stone of a lost ring ,adds glory to the scarp of a
metal.

QUOTE- 3

Losing an unforgettable person, is like losing a part of
the body but still it doesn't becomes a memory.

39. Adila Firoz

Adila Firoz is a final year student pursuing Bachelor's degree in English. She hails from "The God's Own Country" Kerala. She has won numerous accolades in academic, cultural and literary events. She has worked with a couple of anthologies and has explored the literary arena by getting her poems, essays, short stories and articles published. She has also presented research papers in National and International Conferences. Besides, she is a debater, orator, communication trainer, critical thinker and an artist.
Instagram:- @_adila_firoz_

SCENT OF NOSTALGIA
Those times, with golden lustre,
Carried only love, no lust
The unforgettable turns
Enjoyed to the fullest
Challenges were not tiresome
The Journey was tireless
'Cause the delight as incentive sum
Made us not to settle for less
Reminiscing those days
Breathing in the scent of nostalgia
Though lost in thoughts,

It wasn't a loss as such
We couldn't take it as adults
We did pass on the fragrance
To our kids to enjoy
The colour of childhood.

THE UNKNOWN ME
Who am I without
The days I spent with glory
The days I spent with joy
The days I can never forget
Look of innocence
Sparked the days of a child
It looked out to the days
Coming one after the other
To play with friends,
A gala time with family,
Where relationship was only
Friendship and Specialship
I look into myself
See that I differ
From who I used to be
This is the unknown me.

40. Dr. Kanu Tiwari

Dr. Kanu Tiwari is a doctor by profession and a writer and baker by heart. She has participated in 30+ anthologies, published a solo book and has even compiled. She has headed the literary department in her college and has been nominated for various literary awards. She wishes to serve the nation by her profession and change the ideology with her words. Her most prized possessions are her smile, stethoscope and a pen. Connect her on Instagram @drkt_writes

MEMORY
That day; one of a kind,
I played my memories on rewind,
A memory came by,
Well; I don't know why,
A memory I regard,
And with all my heart I guard,
The day I gained
And my life changed
I was seated in a car
And I watched from afar
Someone helping a small boy
Giving some necessities and toys
I made a plan in my mind

And yes, like minded people did a find,
Helping with NGOs was their plan,
With all their heart as much as they can
And I decided to have a role,
And make the world a better place was my goal,
I helped training kids with sewing
And helped my mother with all the kitchen and brewing,
That was the day I truly tasted the rainbow.

MEMORY LANE

Back when I was a girl,
Playing with toys,
Chatting with my bona fide
Life was rozy,
All black and white,
It was either;
Wrong or right.
Sweets and dresses was all I wanted,
Earning money;
Never haunted.
My small family,
Was a haven built well,
A barrier from;
The horrors and hell.
Life was cool,
As a general rule
A stream of happiness,
Flowed and glowed.

Days were spent,
With cheer
Mother's smile,
Took away our fear.
There was my cocoon,
On mother's lap,
My happiness
Was a pat on my back!

41. Dhaanyatha.P

Her name is Dhaanyatha.P from Oddanchatram, Dindigul district, Tamilnadu. She is doing her 11th standard Studies. She is interested in extracurricular activities and also interested in writing poems and Stories too. She is full time busy with her studies and part time writer. She also took a part in many anthologies. She was fond of writing stories. Writing is her passion. These are her works named "Memorable Time," "Unbelievable Memories. It is written by her own experience. Contact her on Instagram @born_403

MEMORABLE TIMES

Time is Precious.

Memories are Unforgettable,

Time is Free, But it is priceless.

You can't own it, But you can use it.

You can't keep it, But you can Spend it.

You can't sale it, But you can share it.

You can't stop it, But you can keep going with it.

Once you've lost it, You can never get it back.

All Great Achievement require Time.

Always Be Patience and don't Waste Time!

UNBELIEVABLE MEMORIES

Life is shorter, Live it.

Love is rare, Grab it.

Anger is bad, Dump it.

Fear is awful, Face it.

Memories are sweet, Cherish it.

Beautiful Memories Are like old friends.

They are Unbelievable Memories.

They may not always Be on your mind,

But they are Forever In your heart.

Memories are Timeless Treasures of the heart.

Time is Precious.

Memories are Unbelievable.

Got Confused ! Read it Again !

42. Anil Kumar Srivastava

He is Anil Srivastava, his birth place and native place is Prayagraj, Uttar Pradesh.

He has completed his graduation from university of Allahabad. At present he is working as a Manager in Limited Company at Nashik in Maharashtra. A poetry book 'मधुशाला ' MADHUSHALA, written by eminent poet Dr. Harivansh Rai Bachchan; inspired to Anil to write poems. Anil's favourite writer is a great Hindi story writer & novelist Munshi PREM CHAND. Gaban, Godan, Karmbhumi is a great Hindi novel, written by Prem Chand. Anil Shrivastava spread awareness among people through his poetry & articles and give a message for adopting good thoughts/traditions and keep far away from bad habits/ evil thoughts. Anil has written >1000 poems and articles.

IN THE MIDDLE OF THE NIGHT
Moon came in my dream
And invited me to hold her.
I held her in my strong arms
Sticking with me, Moon felt happy
And exicted for hang on in my arms forever.
Seeing happy the moon
I forgotten all my pains and a big smile on my face.

IF A WRITER FALLS IN LOVE

He always walk in the heaven with his sweetheart.

Everytime he praise his sweetheart for her beautiful deep

eyes, juicey lips, long curly hair, pulpy cheek, radiant

neck, soft and milky arms, sweet palm,eye eatching low size waist.

He loves her charming, dazzling marvelous appearance

and often want to praise for her lovely, magnificent and cute stylish

walk.

A writer always stay in charm and attraction of gorgeous

look of his sweetheart and create poems for praising his

attractive beloved with plenty of lovely words.

43. Rimpa Sharma

The name of the author is Rimpa Sharma, art is her passion. She has just started exploring herself and the way she looks at the world and feels about it can be seen in her paintings and writings. She's a hard-working and a kind human. She has participated in a numerous writing and painting competitions and came out with a trophy or an award, two of which are won at the Goa University on the theme "women". Her interest in photography leaves the viewers amazed and her creative mind always makes something that is always appreciated, she's been always handling the decoration department at her college events and had been awarded for that as well. She's a down to earth and a nature lover and also loves animals. You can also find her on Instagram on the id @mrignaynie

AAJ KUCH HUA YUN!

Aaj Kuch hua Yun ki hum Ghar laut rahe the .... Man Kiya ki aaj car ki window seat par baithenge!!! Laute huye Kuch hassin nazaron se saamna Hua jinhone kayi binkahi baaten kehdi...! Jab humne aasman ki or Dekha toh pata Chala, ki ek badal humse pehle baagne ki koshish Kar Raha tha! Par Kuch Der baad shayad Woh thak gaya aur piche reh Gaya.....! Humne socha.. Chalo insanose na Sahi hum is badal se toh jite;-) Kuch badal aur bhi the..! Jo khudko Suraj ke rang Mai rang rahe the... Mano Woh rang Milan Ka ho...! Aur woh panchiyan Suraj ki or se ek Katar Mai barat le aa rahi thi... Woh thandi behti hawayen Mano mere Kano Mai Kuch khuspusa rahi thi...!! Aur hum age ja rahe the yaa rasta piche ja Raha tha..? Insabke chalte ek Baat Yaad aa gayi aur Woh thi....ki, yaaron shaam ho aayi hai chalo Ghar laut chalen..! Teri Kami Teri kami khalti toh hai mujhe, phir soachti hu tune hokar bhi kya hi Kar Lena tha? Uss baarish ki shaam, dono ke sar par ek hi chao thi, tera haath mere kaandhe par zarur tha, par Tu mere Saath Nahi tha! Tere diye zakhmon ka dard kuch iss qadar hua ki, Kisi or ke war ka hum par koi asar hi nahi hua. Meri Orr tera woh ek beparwah sa ravaiyaa..., Par Tu Sahi tha, mujh Jaise ki parwah, bhala koi beparwah kyun hi karega? Tera Dil narm jarur hai, bas Jo uski banawat, pathar ki hai, toh Mai ek pathar se Dil ki Aas kaise rakhti? Pyaar ek tarfa tujhse kuch iss hadd tak hua ki wakt Ka chalta Har ek kanta mujhe tere Karib le jata. Kambakht Dil ko hazar dafa samjhaya ki ishq tujhse Nahi, par tere hone ke ehsaas se hai. Aaj bhi, Teri Kami khalti toh hai mujhe, phir soachti Hu ki tune hokar bhi kya hi Kar Lena tha?

44. Diya Mishra

Diya Mishra is from Prayagraj, Uttar Pradesh. She is 13 years old and study in 9th standard. She came up from a family of six. Her grandfather, Mr.Virendra Mishra is whom she idolize and he is the one who inspired her to start writing. Her hobbies are Dancing, Reading, Public speaking, Writing and theater. Her goal is to become an entrepreneur and to step in the lm industry. She is and polyglot and can speak 6 languages that includes Hindi, English, Sanskrit, French, German and Japanese, also she is a linguist in Hindi and English. She writes short stories, poems and scripts of short lms in three languages that are Hindi, English and Sanskrit. She loves to read and investigate about the culture, tradition, mythology and history of different countries. Her will is to learn more about quantum mechanics and innovate something in that field.

SEASONAL MEMORIES

When I closed my eyes, I could feel the rain,
Someone's sorrow, someone's pain, or it is the joy of the rain!
Laughing and chiming, when I saw her first day,
In a white gown ladle with illuminating snowflakes.
I wanted to be her prince and make her my princess,

But, the only thing that was left was her memories in the
rain.
Seasons passed and, now the lonely winter came,
Passing through the streets,
Streets covered with a blanket of snowy wind,
Listening to the jingles, I slew my loneliness;
Neither the kin nor stranger remembered me by my
name.
When I was passing by the woods,
I saw a dear dwell under the pinewood,
I could felt the warmth through the hearth,
That bring back memories,
The memories bring back- memories bring back me.
The days of my boyhood,
When I knew to cry,
When I kenned to smile,
When I knew to be satisfied with my family!

45. Ishita Saxena

This is Ishita Saxena from Bareilly,She has been Written Since 2Years, And Written her words in many books as a coauthor. She also Written Some her words in a Magazine by 'THE INKSCRIBBLERS' community. Even She opened a writting community named 'ADMIRE OF ILLUSION.'
Instagram:- ishu_deepthinker

MEMORIES COME BACK TO LIFE!
When! We become Strong Again, Explain the all the matter to The Heart' & Said that whatever happened for a good reason Nothing is Bad, Even You are Safe:) When we get a little closer to someone else ... & We start smile again ... When We start liking ourselves. When We star talking to otherselves... When We want to move on....! Actually! Memories Come to life All the time....

THE OCEAN IS THE POEM
Teachs Us; Never Ending Love, The Reactions of Happiness and Grief Up and Down. Do not back down from Any difculties Face all the difculties, These are some Special Lessons of life... Show Your Strength & Make some noise by Your Success & Never stop Jzt let

it be..

46. Dhairya M. Thakkar

Dhairya M. Thakkar is a 17 years old lad from Ghatkopar West, Mumbai. Apart from a XII Grade Commerce Student, he is also a Rapper, Writer, Tabla Player & A Podcast Host. He has close to 500 Monthly Listeners on Spotify. He is a CA aspirant as well. He has contributed as a Co Author, as a Compiler and as a PH in multiple anthologies. He has penned down multiple poems, articles & stories which are published in multiple anthologies. He also works as a Content Writer for an NGO. He enjoys Reading Books and playing chess is his favourite passtime. Love for His Legacy is the reason of his hustle.

2:00 A.M. MEMORIES

Life is a roller coaster,
It has it's ups & downs;
Sometimes we laugh,
Sometimes we frown;
Life is a circle, what goes around, then comes around;
So, your actions, will someday, surely rebound.
Living life is difficult, facing problems in every way;
Problems should be solved & aren't meant to stay away;
"Find a Way OR Fade Away", they say; but
When we face problems, it's difficult to hit the hay.

Thode 2:00 AM sessions, guilty thoughts gets piled;
Many a times, it's just a step sway from suicide;
Few wounds on heart are deep, and it's can't be revived;
Plus when depression comes in, it closes doors of hitting high.

47. Samyuktha

This is Samyuktha Sathies Kumar, A sixteen-year-old aspiring writer and compiler from India who started her writing journey in 2018. She is currently studying in grade 12 [science stream]. She has co-authored many books and has compiled a few books.
Instagram:- 3xclusivedreamer3

MEMORIES
Those tapes replay In front of me
So blurry but yet lovely.

MEMORIES OF YOU AND ME
You and me were playing tag
In the middle of woods
With carefree smiles allover
With no worries or grudges in our hearts
With nothing but a happy heart
Just enjoying our lives In our own little world.

LONELY WITH YOU
Those weekends
When I was lonely

Together with you
While feeling the warmth
Of our memories.
It was cozy
It was heartwarming
I wish we could go back
And stay close to each other.

48. Rushabh Kharade

He is Rushabh Kharade, a person who loves to experiments in life a lot and now he trying to bring peace to souls.

Instagram:- @Kharade_sahab

BAHUT KUCH

Bahut kuchh sochta Hun main

Per kabhi kehe nahin pata

Kaafi log hone ke baad bhi

Main unke sath rahe nahin pata

Kafi bato ke baad bhi

Main unhen apna kahe nahin pata

Bahar se main hasta dikhta per

Andar se mein rota hu

Bohot kuch bhara hua andar hai

Mai r bhi pura khali hu

Main roj thoda thoda khud Ko khota hu

CHOOSE WISELY

Everytime something good or bad happens we blame on some or the other person or thing for it. what if? we didn't chose that person or a thing. what if? we didn't took that decision when something good or something bad was experienced by you. what would be the consequences then? Others didn't make choices for us It's us who makes choices so if something bad happened then its also because of our choices and if something good happened then also it's because our choices.

The End